Managing Information as a Resource

Central Computer and
Telecommunications Agency

LONDON: HMSO

First published 1990

ISBN 0 11 330529 X

For further information on this publication please contact:

Barry Older or Mark Sudan
Strategic Issues Group
Central Computer & Telecommunications Agency
Riverwalk House
157–161 Millbank
London SW1P 4RT

CONTENTS

1 Introduction

1.1 Background

This guidance is about managing information as a resource and follows on from the HM Treasury (RC2) paper of December 1987 under the title 'Managing Information as a Resource'. The guidance is designed for use by the officials in departments who are tasked with the management of information. A Management Overview has been published under the auspices of HM Treasury which addresses senior managers, responsible for all departmental information services, their organisation and staffing. It contains much of the material in Chapters 1 and 2, and briefly describes the coverage of this guidance.

This guidance should be read in conjunction with the guidance on Information Systems (IS) Strategy contained in IS Guide A2: Strategic Planning for Information Systems. Also relevant is the Management Personnel Office (MPO) series of guidelines and notes on Records Management, which provide detailed guidance for Departmental Records Officers (DROs). See Annex 5 for sources of further information.

The material in the guidance has been drawn from many sources, but mainly from experience gained in departments in recent years. The authors are grateful to the many officials, academics and consultants who have contributed their ideas, experience and knowledge to the preparation of this document.

1.2 Information is a Resource

The dictionary defines a resource as:

- a means of supplying a want
- stock that can be drawn on; or
- a means for support.

In manufacturing industry the three main resources are:

- labour
- capital
- raw materials.

In Government, the equivalents are:

- personnel
- finance
- information.

Personnel and finance are easily recognised and treated by departments as resources. Information is not currently perceived or treated in the same way. If we take a resource to be something which:

1 is **essential** to the **achievement of business objectives** and operation of the department

2 can be obtained by the department, at a **cost**

3 even where it is not essential, can be employed, alone or with other resources, to further the achievement of the department's **aims and objectives**

then information has all these properties.

1 It is **essential**; the business of government is dependent upon information to such an extent that no department could continue to operate without its sources of information.

2 It has **a cost**; departments devote about half of their administrative budget to information handling activities of one kind or another:

- collection, (eg collecting trade statistics)
- internal and external dissemination (messengers, advisory services, data networks, publications, etc)
- processing and storage (paper records, microfiche, computers)
- archiving and disposal (record review, confidential waste)
- skilled staff used on all of the activities above.

3 It is used in all Government departments and at all levels within departments to assist in the achievement of relevant **aims and objectives**:

- At the policy level, information is needed to help develop policies and plans, to answer Ministers' correspondence, to handle Parliamentary Questions or as material for debates in Parliament.

— For managers, the need to ensure efficient and effective use of money and manpower, etc, information about performance and achievement; as well as helping target effort on areas of greatest need.

— In some cases, information is the sole output of a Government department (eg Central Office of Information, Central Statistical Office, Office of Population Censuses and Surveys).

— For operational decisions information is used on such matters as the level of grant payable (eg Department of Social Security, Department of Trade and Industry, Ministry of Agriculture Food and Fisheries), or the level of revenue due (eg HM Customs & Excise, Inland Revenue).

Information therefore possesses the properties that are associated with resources:

- it is essential to every aspect of Government business
- it incurs costs (often hidden) in collection, storage, processing, etc
- it belongs to the organisation as a whole.

1.3 Benefits of Information Management

Effective use of information adds value to all the activities of departments. It can:

- improve the quality of information for policy-makers and planners
- enable more effective discharge of operational functions and higher quality of service to the public
- produce more accurate, cost-effective management information
- reduce expenditure on the collection, communication and storage of unnecessary data
- better focus IS investment.

The information which departments hold may also allow them to exploit wider business opportunities, the benefits from which would outweigh the cost of the resources necessary to achieve them.

Inefficient use of information wastes money. Many examples of inefficiency can be found including:

- information which is collected but not needed
- information stored long after it is needed
- useful information which is inaccessible to potential users
- information disseminated more widely than is necessary
- inefficient methods used to collect, analyse, store and retrieve information
- collection of the same basic information by more than one group of people in the same department
- duplicated storage of the same basic information.

By recognising these problems and taking the appropriate action to correct them, managers can reduce their information handling costs. Given the size of government expenditure on information handling, quite small improvements in the efficient use of information will result in very large potential savings across the Service. For example, guidance produced under the Records Management Programme has resulted in substantial savings in departments over the past three years.

You can make more effective use of information by:

- specifying the needs for information (including its content, quality and timeliness) within an organisational process
- identifying the most appropriate sources of information to meet those needs
- identifying the most appropriate mechanism for the delivery of this information
- establishing the procedures to allow data from two or more sources to be brought together to provide information at the point of need.

Provision of information to users, as a regular activity, should be complemented by information services which are easily accessible and allow users to find the information they need with the minimum difficulty and minimum intervention by skilled specialists.

2 Department policy and organisation

2.1 How information fits into the management framework

As with the management of other resources, the need for information must be firmly based on the business needs of the department. It is important to make the links between business and resource requirements explicit.

The normal sequence of activities to ensure this is as follows:

- define the purpose of the organisation and establish its general aims supported by specific objectives
- plan how best to carry these aims and objectives forward, having regard to the "outside" environment within which it operates
- acquire the necessary financial, personnel, information and other resources which it requires to implement those plans
- put the plans (possibly amended in the light of actual resources obtained) into operation
- measure the organisation's achievement against its objectives, plans and resource allocations
- make whatever changes are necessary in the light of actual performance against objectives.

Figure 1 (not an organisation chart) illustrates how the first two of these activities at senior management level govern the operations of the specialist resource management services.

Within such a logical structure, information management is linked naturally with the business of the department. Information management also has implications for the departmental functions responsible for different aspects of information provision. Individually each provider can make a worthwhile contribution to the achievement of a department's aims, but acting together and exploiting each other's strengths and expertise they will form the basis for the realisation of the full benefits of information management. It is important therefore that they are seen, and see themselves, as having the same common objectives and that their activities are co-ordinated to make best use of the specialised skills they possess.

Departments differ greatly in function, organisation and the ways in which their information services operate. There is therefore no single "recipe" for introducing information management successfully. Experience shows, however, that three things are necessary:

- top management must be committed to the principles of information management (paragraph 2.2)
- policy and objectives for information management must be defined (paragraph 2.3)
- an individual or unit must be given clear responsibility for carrying out that policy (paragraph 2.4).

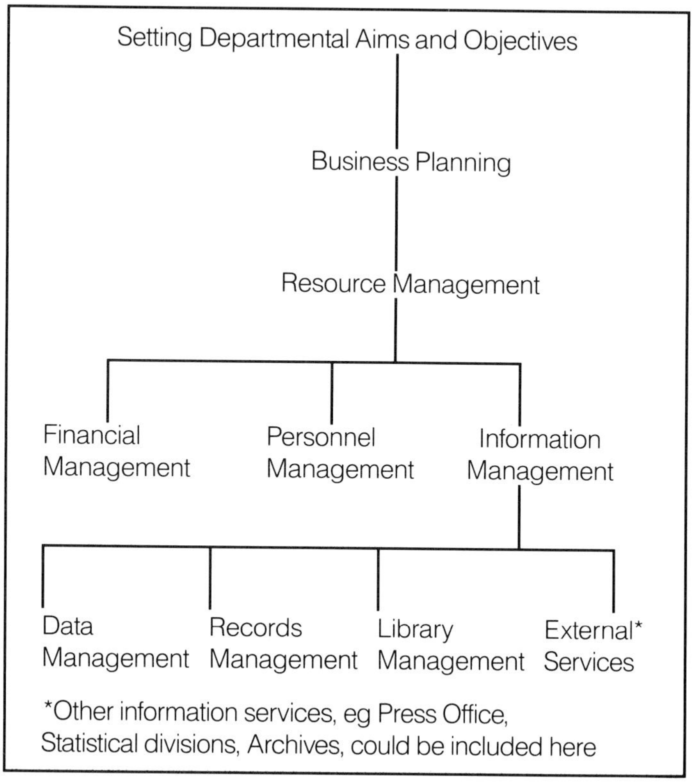

Figure 1: Managing the department's resources

2.2 The Role of Top Management

Top management commitment is vital because:

- in most departments the reporting lines for the different information service functions meet only at a very senior level, usually the PEO
- resources must be allocated to the new information management function, recognising that a return on the investment will be relatively slow
- the introduction of information management has far-reaching consequences throughout the department, and like any process of change, needs high level support.

Introducing departmental-wide information management will require changes in organisation and culture. Bringing about such changes is not a trivial task.

Information management, in common with all other resource management action, carries with it considerable "up-front" costs which are only repaid over a relatively lengthy period of gradually improving performance. (Consider the Financial Management Initiative or the Personnel Work Action Programme.) It is difficult today to quantify the actual benefits secured as a direct result of these initiatives, but no department would contemplate operating without disciplined accounting or expect to attract and retain staff without proper personnel management. Such things are accepted as essential parts of the organisational infrastructure.

Information management should similarly become part of the accepted culture of a department; it will not do so without effort at all levels. The focus for this effort will come from the information manager and the information management unit (paragraph 2.4), but it will not succeed without the organisational clout which only top management commitment can provide.

2.3 Policy and Objectives for Information Management

Clearly articulated policies and objectives will help to ensure that throughout the department there is a common understanding about responsibilities for information and about what needs to be done to meet them. Ideally, these policies will have been defined in a departmental IS Strategy as described in IS Guide A2: Strategic Planning for Information Systems.

Policies and objectives, and the actions required for achieving them, will be specific to departments' circumstances and nature of the businesses they carry on. Experience gained in government and elsewhere suggests that policies should:

- contain an explicit statement from top management that information is a vital departmental resource, and will be managed as such
- draw attention to the responsibilities of individual staff for information
- identify the individual(s) responsible for driving the policies through to implementation.

If the department has no IS Strategy a **short initial review** has generally been found to be useful to define the precise nature of the policies and to show how they should be implemented, with the identifiable benefits of doing so. Implementation can involve some very small-scale tasks to simplify existing information management arrangements, (eg the transfer of selected information from one unit to another). Other steps will lead to more fundamental changes which will require significant time, effort and resources to carry them through. Legal restrictions on the use of information, commercial sensitivity, confidentiality of personal data and national security must all be taken into account when proposals to extend access and use of information are considered.

The information management policy statement could include explicit reference to:

- Public Records Acts
- Official Secrets Act
- Copyright, Designs and Patents Act 1988
- Data Protection Act; and
- any other legislation restricting the use of information peculiar to the department.

For further information you will find it useful to refer to the CCTA IS Guide C4: Security and Privacy.

In Annex 1 you will find examples illustrating the approach taken by three different departments. Within these examples specific techniques to assist in the tasks of information management are incorporated in the policies, but other approaches using a variety of techniques are equally as valid.

2.4 The information management unit

It is essential that an individual, or group of individuals, is given clear responsibility for carrying through the department's agreed policies for information management.

Although this is likely to mean new posts wholly dedicated to information management work, it does not necessarily imply a need to recruit any extra staff. For most departments the roles of the information manager and his/her team could most easily and logically be taken on by staff already working in either the information service area (eg, in the library, records management or information technology) or elsewhere (eg, management services or policy branches) who understand the issues. Each department should adopt the arrangement that best suits its own circumstances.

Whatever the composition of the information management unit, it will be responsible for organising, and possibly carrying out, the tasks necessary to achieve the continuous management of the information resource. These tasks will include:

- taking part in the formulation and review of the departmental IS Strategy (see IS Guide A2) by:
  - contributing to the Strategy Study
  - providing a member of the IS Steering Committee, the IS Planning Secretariat, and the Strategy Study Team
  - helping to define the Management and Technical Policies (in which the department's policies for co-ordinating the provision of information are defined)
  - carrying out implementation planning
- promoting the principles and benefits of information management, departmental policy and objectives and a general awareness of the subject; and obtaining commitment throughout the department

- identifying information needs throughout the department
- creating a body of knowledge on the information available within the department, where and how it may be accessed, and its contribution to the day-to-day operational tasks
- advising on the methods of acquiring information not currently available within the department (eg external databases, market research, library services, etc)
- advising on information management issues which are specific to the needs of the department. For example:
  - charging for IT services, Records Management and Library services
  - the exploitation of departmental information which might be more widely 'tradeable'
  - education and training for line managers and information specialists, etc.

The unit should also set targets for the first few years and indicate how progress against them will be reported back to top management during this period.

It should be closely linked with the IS Planning Secretariat and report directly to a senior official, perhaps the Principal Establishment Officer. The unit's responsibilities would encompass all the tasks described in Chapter 3, though many tasks would be delegated to specialist staff outside the unit. The prime objective should be the co-ordination of all information handling services and processes within the department, liaising with the IS Steering Committee, Management Services, IT Directorates, Statistical services, the Departmental Records Officer (and Chief Registrar where that is a separate post), Librarians, the Press Office etc, all of whom will contribute in their various ways to the information management function.

The unit will need to bring together experience and skill from a range of disciplines and specialisms across the department in order to:

- win and retain the confidence of groups of people who have a far greater knowledge of the business area under investigation;
- extract, from a plethora of facts and opinion gathered, the key issues which need to be addressed; and
- think imaginatively about these often complex and inter-related issues.

2.5 Work in departments to date

Departments are approaching information management in different ways:

- in HMSO the Departmental Records Officer (DRO) has seen the need to expand his area of responsibility for Public Records by becoming more involved in other information services and has made proposals for a co-ordinated information management programme;
- in the Training Agency the main thrust has come from the Information Technology (IT) area, in an attempt to relate IT development more closely to business planning. The Information Manager, who reports to the head of the IT Division, chairs a consultative group which includes economists, statisticians and other information services staff from the wider Training Agency community;
- in MOD a qualified librarian is now working in IT planning, and in PSA and DTI others have taken over responsibility for Records Management;
- DTI and MAFF have conducted information audits;
- and CCTA and DTI have compiled thesauri for describing the content of registered files and computer files.

All these developments are useful building blocks towards the full integration of information services and co-ordinated departmental information management.

At the centre, CCTA's latest guidance on Information Systems Strategy (in IS Guide A2) is designed to make departmental Business Management aware of their responsibilities to ensure effective planning of information systems, of which IT is only a part. The Public Record Office (PRO) is actively working to make departments more aware of electronic records as public records (in the same sense as are registered files and other papers).

Other more detailed examples are described at Annex 1.

3 The tasks of Information Management

3.1 Overview

Figure 2 shows the broad picture of information management and its activities. The remainder of this section contains descriptions of these activities. A few of the specialised techniques required for their accomplishment are considered in Annex 2, whilst a wider choice of such techniques are described in IS Guide A2: Strategic Planning for Information Systems.

The underlying questions that need to be addressed to enable effective information management are:

- what are the department's business aims and objectives?
- what information is needed to support those aims?
- what information is available in the department?
- are there differences between needs and provision?
- what needs to be done to match needs with provision?
- how is information best delivered to users?
- is further exploitation of information viable?

Many of these tasks are not new, but have seldom been applied to the totality of a department's information resources. There is a great deal of expertise and help available within departments' information services which can contribute to their achievement. The tasks are all continuous, though some of them require periodic review, probably as part of the IS Strategy review process. There is a logical sequence to be followed in order to get started and that is the order in which the activities are described in this chapter, approximately from top left to bottom right of Figure 2.

The need to manage the information resource centrally does not mean that individual officers do not need to worry about it. On the contrary, one of the aims of information management must be to spread an awareness of every line manager's responsibility for the efficient and effective use of information and the information services.

3.2 Information Management in relation to Business and IS Strategies

CCTA advises every department to plan all its information systems (both IT and non-IT) through a high-level planning process which produces the "IS Strategy". IS Guide A2 describes this process. The IS Strategy is a rolling 5–10 year plan, subjected to frequent review. It is tied to the Public Expenditure Survey (PES) and the annual estimates. Based on the policies laid down in the Strategy, individual functions in the department produce their own 12–18 month 'Tactical Plan' (described, for the IT function, in IS

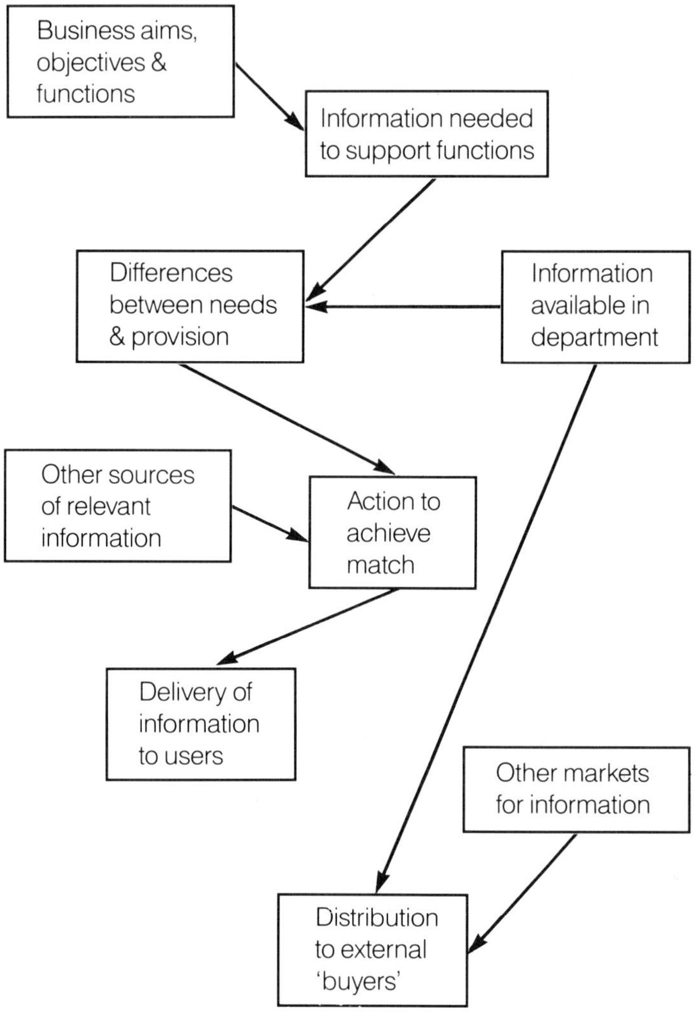

Figure 2 Information management: information and activities

Guide A3: Computer and Office Systems Planning) which shows how they will resource and carry through those parts of the Strategy for which they are responsible.

Information management is a key part of this process of planning departmental information systems, and is best carried out in that context. However, where formal strategic planning, with its attendant IS Steering Committee and IS Planning Secretariat, does not yet exist in the department, information management should still be pursued.

The IS Strategy itself depends on an existing, higher level of planning: a Corporate or Business Strategy. That Business Strategy should articulate the department's business aims and functions over a specific period of time, and is therefore a vital starting point when planning the co-ordinated management of the department's information. When a business strategy has not been formally articulated, or is not fully developed, top management must be encouraged to articulate, as explicitly as possible, the general aims towards which the department is directing its efforts, and the specific objectives it intends to achieve. Without the clear statement of corporate purpose there will be no coherent basis for building and managing the department's information systems.

3.3 What are the department's business aims and objectives?

The starting point for information management, as for other departmental management functions, must be **an understanding of the department's business, its aims and objectives,** (see definitions in glossary, Annex 6), which should be available from business planning documents or the department's IS Strategy, and how these are translated into the functions it performs. Unless these business aims and objectives are clear and not in dispute it will not be possible to judge what information the department needs, or how best to provide it. This is not just a question of listing all the possible aims and objectives. In a world where resources are limited a department must decide priorities so that its new information management unit can concentrate on the types of information most needed to discharge departmental business functions. Similarly new requirements for information must be anticipated, so that they can be met early enough to be useful.

As well as identifying objectives and priorities, it is necessary to analyse the department's business as it currently stands. Modelling techniques such as those referred to in Annex 2, and IS Guide A2, can be used to clarify what may be complex real world situations. These techniques include:

- representation of the department's functional and organisational structure
- charts and tables illustrating how the different attributes of the business interrelate.

Techniques for representing information flows within the department (see paragraph 3.4.2) are also referred to in the documents cited in the previous paragraph.

3.4 Information needed to support those aims

Where the department has an IS Strategy, as described in IS Guide A2 , its information requirements will have been defined within it. (However the Strategy will require reviewing to ensure that it still meets business needs.) If an IS Strategy has not been developed you will need to undertake the following tasks.

3.4.1 Defining information requirements

The most satisfactory approach to defining information needs is by studying the business functions of the department and by thinking through the kind of information that is needed to carry them out. Ideally, information needs should be defined first at the most general, top level across the whole department, and then progressively at lower levels. This top down method ensures a coherent picture across the whole organisation.

3.4.2 Analysing information flows

Detailed analysis of information needs involves examining each function within the business area in turn to determine what information is needed to support those functions, and what information they themselves produce. By tabulating the results of this analysis you can identify:

- where information is common to several different functions
- where information is produced
- where it needs to be communicated between functions

- information currently collected but not required
- information required but not collected
- inadequate information (eg late delivery, inappropriate media, etc)
- the data from which information is produced.

The results are discussed with business managers at each step to ensure the nature of the work has been fully understood and that business managers are happy with them. Where functions are well-defined and understood, and derived from centrally agreed aims and objectives the task is a great deal easier, but there is still value in going back to basics to check out the completeness of the information needs defined.

Remember that the department will change as time goes on. After the initial exercise, the analysis of information needs should be reviewed periodically, to ensure that it remains accurate. Parts of the picture should be redefined as changes occur in the nature of the department's business eg. as the result of the introduction of new legislation or regulations, or when significant staff or organisational changes are made. Changes of this sort can affect the information needed and the priorities for meeting those needs.

The way in which information requirements are described is significant. The terminology used must be the same as that used for describing existing information in the information inventory (see paragraph 3.5.1), so that the two may be compared. (see paragraph 3.5.2, and Annex 2).

3.5 What information is available in the department?

Where a department has an IS Strategy much of the work described below will already have been undertaken. If not, it should be undertaken as part of establishing or reviewing an IS Strategy.

3.5.1 Making an information inventory

Before you can assess how far known needs are being met you will need to have a clear picture of the existing state of information systems (paper-based and technology-based) within the department, and the information they contain. It is essential to carry out an information audit in order to prepare a detailed inventory of all existing information.

The resulting inventory will contain the following:

1 Details of all information held in the department:

- what information is held (its subject matter or content)
- where it is located and in what form
- who manages and maintains it
- how it can be accessed and what are the present trends (eg, towards greater office automation, or increased use of senior management support systems)
- how effective the information systems are in supporting business and policy aims, objectives and priorities (current and future).

2 Details of the department's information systems:

- current major assets
- equipment used to support existing information systems
- objectives, functions and processes supported by these systems
- the resources used to operate, maintain and develop them
- where applicable, the software tools to develop and support them.

Where an IS Strategy exists there should be details of existing information systems, which you should check for accuracy. In the absence of a Strategy, in order to compile an inventory you will need to refer to the existing records of the information services, existing information systems documentation, reports and information gained from interviews, and obtain agreement from individuals and relevant groups on the current status of the information systems.

Conducting an information audit is an extensive and time-consuming task which should be planned properly and resourced adequately. Careful thought should be given to the level and calibre of staff needed, and the time it is likely to take to complete the work. The success of the exercise will depend very largely upon the co-operation of those being asked to provide the relevant information: they should therefore be informed about why it is taking place.

Before work begins you should:

- ensure that adequate publicity has been given to the information providers about the preparation of the inventory and its purpose within the overall framework of information management
- decide how the data collected by the information audit is to be organised and stored; what software (if any) is needed to do these things
- ensure that enough time and resources are available for reviewing and evaluating the data collected, especially where it is necessary to ask the provider for further clarification
- consider how the inventory will be maintained; whether the information audit is likely to need to be repeated in order to keep the total picture up-to-date; whether this can be incorporated into any wider cyclical review process.

The cost of the work involved must be balanced against the immediate and likely future benefits which the inventory will bring to the department. To be of real value, the inventory will need to be presented in the right form so that it can be understood by all categories of information user. It will also need to be reviewed and updated periodically to reflect changes in business, functions, organisation and methods of working.

Business managers must, for their part, take responsibility for notifying the information manager/ unit (see paragraph 2.4) whenever they plan to create or take on a new data collection, or whenever they decide to withdraw one from use. They should also be encouraged to check the inventory to ensure that any new material does not duplicate, either wholly or in part, data collections held elsewhere in the department.

3.5.2 Describing Information

The information described in the information inventory will be widely distributed and will be contained in a wide range of media:

- registered files

- books
- periodicals
- official reports
- computer databases, etc.

The inventory will need to be organised carefully and the information groupings recorded in it will need to be described consistently so that enquirers can find what they want and can recognise relevant material when it is retrieved.

Description implies the use of a clear and generally accepted set of terms—a standard or "common" language—for representing the ideas contained within all information sources, an example is the standard cataloguing rules used by librarians. In a typical department, the techniques used for describing information must:

- be capable of being applied consistently to a variety of media
- be understood by, and accessible to, all users in the organisation, whatever their individual specialisms and wherever they happen to be working
- enable all users to identify, locate and retrieve the information that they require with the minimum of searching.

Much of the information will already have been ordered and described by the different specialist information services within the department:

- library
- records management; and
- IT Directorate.

However the terms used by the specialists do differ and although they should be derived from the nature of the business of the department there is often little correspondence between them.

Some departmental information is not formally described or organised according to any particular standard, or at all in some cases. For example, documents created in word-processing systems may have quite meaningless names, making them inaccessible to anyone other than the author. Discipline in the use of naming standards has to be enforced in systems where documents are created if those documents are to be retained in their original medium and to have lasting value. The Public Record Acts do not only cover paper records; all officially produced "documents" may have historical value and should be considered for permanent preservation at the Public Record Office.

In the case of personal collections of papers the situation is worse still. We often find piles rather than files. The 'owner' probably assumes that the papers have no value to anybody else, and that he or she will know where to find something next time it is needed. Even at a local level this can create problems when officers are absent from the office, or on leave.

Librarians are probably a department's most skilled information describers. Where no common description language or thesaurus of terms exists for the department, their help and advice in compiling one should be sought by other information workers. There are also well-developed naming techniques used in registries, and in database administration.

Annex 2 discusses various methods of organising and describing information.

3.6 Other potential sources of information

A good deal of the information that may be relevant to a department's business is likely to be found in, or be available from, external sources and you should be aware of this. Some of the sources for external information are listed in Annex 3.

3.7 Are there differences between needs and provision?

Having identified the information required to support the business functions of the department, you should then assess the effectiveness of the current information systems (both paper-based and technology-based) as detailed in the information inventory, for example:

- to what extent do they directly support business and policy priorities?
- how efficient are they in terms of the effort required to use and maintain them?

- are they sufficiently flexible to meet changing business needs and user requirements?
- are systems provided efficiently and effectively?

From this assessment you should be able to identify gaps or deficiencies (misalignments) in the quality of information supplied in support of the department's business functions and, depending upon their significance to the business, allocate the appropriate priority to their resolution.

3.8 Action to achieve a match between needs and resources

Appropriate ways of resolving the misalignments must be decided, either by internal provision or by acquiring from some external source. An awareness of the external sources of relevant information is thus also required, details of which are often known by librarians.

Redundant information should be closely examined to see whether the information can safely be disposed of. For example, departments often keep information which is not required for any operation of the department, but solely for the purpose of answering Parliamentary Questions. Whilst it is acknowledged that briefing the Minister is a legitimate function of policy divisions, departments should look carefully at the costs of collecting and retaining information which serves no other purpose.

Business managers (users of information and information services) and system designers must have access to the departmental inventory of information stocks, to avoid unnecessary duplication of information in new systems. Existing stocks should be used wherever practicable, though new forms of storage, processing or presentation, etc. may be required, as demanded by the new uses to which it is to be put.

3.9 Delivery of information to users

At all levels, information systems must be designed within the context of the work people do. Only by considering how the information is to be used can we make sensible judgements about the best means of delivering and presenting it.

Information is acquired, generated, distributed and stored by users in a variety of ways. Some information, especially internally generated correspondence, is stored mainly in registered files, which may be retained in the user's desk drawer while in action, in the local registry for less frequent reference, and eventually in some remote store when it is unlikely to be needed often or quickly. Computer databases have traditionally been the repository for large collections of numeric information and statistics, but are being increasingly used for textual material which requires sophisticated manipulation or simultaneous multiple access. The **library** is the traditional home of books and periodicals and possibly departmental reports. The sphere of activity of the library is expanding to include less passive information services, with current awareness bulletins and access through to external information services. Other published material is **collected by individuals** or provided by **circulation of newspapers,** etc. Departments are developing extensive communications networks and **electronic mailing systems** for passing around all kinds of internal "papers".

Much information is also exchanged orally in meetings and **committees** or by **telephone,** both for internal information and in contacts with industry and the general public.

All these means of handling information are valuable in different circumstances. The choice depends on the purpose to which the information is put, who the user is, and the activity he or she is engaged in when they use it. We know that computers can communicate faster than the mail and hold vast amounts of data. However, we cannot automatically assume that more rapid delivery or the ability to store much more information is inherently valuable and we must consider carefully whether such developments are cost-justified, what other means are available to us and what the advantages and disadvantages of using these other means might be in relation to the jobs we are carrying out and the customers we serve.

3.10 Exploiting information:

Information collected by and generated within an organisation has value to that organisation, but it may also have value to other organisations or individuals, depending on their own business requirements. Departments could exchange their information inventories as a first step in identifying other governmental customers external to the department.

Information is a commodity which can be bought and sold like any other. In common with other raw materials, it can increase in value at different stages of processing. Value can be added in a number of different ways:

- through greater accessibility;
- by placing information alongside other information;
- by appropriate structuring and storage;
- through trading;
- through re-use in new or different contexts.

All these means of adding value to information increasingly depend upon computer storage and retrieval. More sophisticated IT and communications systems have opened up opportunities for easier, quicker and cheaper exchange and distribution of information.

3.10.1 Tradeable Information Initiative

The Tradeable Information Initiative was launched by DTI in 1986 in response to a report to the Prime Minister published in 1983 by the IT Advisory Panel (ITAP) entitled 'Making a business of information'. The ITAP Report recommended that the economic importance of tradeable information should be recognised, opportunities for growth should be enhanced, and that the UK information industry should be stimulated through the release of Government-held information.

The Tradeable Information Initiative is concerned with encouraging the supply of Government-held information (statistics, company data, patents details, licensing records and news information services etc) to commercial concerns in the information sector. The intention is that these firms will then create public-access information retrieval services in response to market demand. There are three specific objectives:

1 to stimulate the UK information market on a commercial basis

2 to promote efficiency and competitiveness in the wider economy through the use of commercial electronic information services

3 in the context of Government–held tradeable information, to make as much information as possible available to private sector information services.

3.10.2 Identifying tradeable information

To help departments to identify and record the commercially-exploitable information that they hold, DTI have produced a set of Tradeable Information Policy Guidelines. These are concerned only with information which the private sector will turn into electronic information services, but a department may, of course, hold exploitable data in paper-based as well as machine-readable form.

To identify and assess the potential commercial value of any information it holds, a department should in the first place carry out a thorough information audit (see Annex 2). DTI's Guidelines contain practical advice on undertaking such an exercise. They also deal with issues such as Crown Copyright, costs and charges and the framing of contracts.

3.10.3 Publication

Opportunities exist for departments to exploit the wider potential of the information they hold by publishing it commercially.

It is up to each department to decide whether any of its information is likely to be of general public interest, and what sort of demand there will be for it in a professionally produced and marketed form. A department may, of course, already have an established product on the market, and simply need help in improving the text or presentation in order to increase sales. Alternatively, it may have identified the commercial potential of a particular information source for the first time, but lack the resources and expertise to develop a marketable product. Either way, it can seek advice on how to proceed from HMSO, which, in addition to its other functions, provides a comprehensive publishing service to government departments and other public sector bodies.

Any department intending to publish official information for sale should bear in mind that, whether it is HMSO or a commercial publishing company who gets the contract, Crown Copyright remains vested in the Controller of HMSO, and his approval will be needed before publication can take place.

A brief description of the publication services offered by HMSO is at Annex 4.

3.11 Management Information — a special case

One function which exists at all levels in a department is management: management of business operations, management of central services, management of particular resources, management of policy functions, etc. Much effort has gone into defining the information and information systems needed to support management (Management Information Systems, MIS) in recent years, with varying degrees of success.

Management Information is a special category of information.

On the one hand much of it differs from the kind of corporate information which supports the carrying out of business functions directly; it is needed, rather, by managers of individual units (and their own managers at adjacent levels) for tasks such as monitoring the performance of their units.

On the other hand there will be a considerable body of management information, relating to the department as a whole, which is needed by managers who have responsibilities across the whole organisation:

- information needed to check overall performance
- information about planning assumptions, priorities, and business direction, decided by top management
- information about results (of the kind found in the Annual Report).

The basic activities of management at any level are much the same and can be illustrated with the activity model shown in Figure 3. The model shows that all the activities are inter-dependent (the arrows indicate a dependence and the wavy arrow shows a possible link into any of the other activities) and therefore the management task and its supporting information system cannot work properly unless they are complete. A manager at any level must:

- know what he or she is trying to achieve
- translate that into a plan showing how to achieve it and resources needed to achieve it
- arrange for the plan to be put into effect
- measure the results and exercise control of the whole operation.

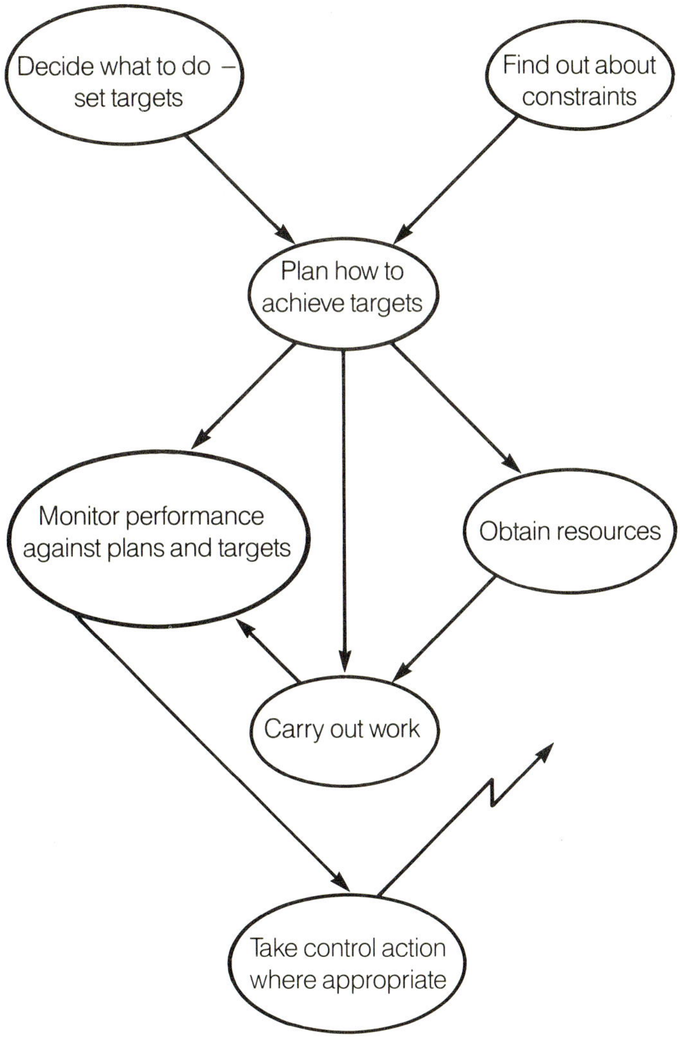

Figure 3 Activity model

Management information, as derived from this model, should consist of information about:

a objectives, targets, expectations of performance,

b constraints, limits on budget, discretion,

(both of which are necessary for planning purposes);

c performance or achievement of objectives, etc,

d resources consumed

(which are required for control of the operations and feedback into planning).

Conventionally, attention has mostly concentrated on categories c and d, and on information required for reporting back up the line, rather than for local control purposes. Every manager should be assessing his/her own unit's performance, judging whether it represents value for money, and intervening when necessary. Value for money judgements require the manager to know what the unit has achieved and what it has cost.

Often far too much information is reported up. Reporting by exception enjoyed a brief vogue, but is dependent upon realistic standards and targets being set in advance. This is especially difficult when the nature of the business is not constant. A few well-chosen indicators should be adequate to demonstrate to the next highest level of management whether the unit is functioning satisfactorily or not. When it is not then questions will be asked and more detail demanded. Success might be judged against past performance or against estimates, as appropriate.

Information to be reported up the line should be defined by the manager reported to, and derived from his/her view of what is critically important about the lower level operations. Frequency and method of reporting will be for local negotiation.

4 Conclusion

Information is a vital resource for every organisation, like personnel and finance, and none more so than for those in government.

Information is essential, no government department could operate without it. Departments devote about half of their administrative budget on handling information so it obviously has a cost. It therefore requires managing in much the same way as the other key resources.

As a starting point you need to ensure that:

- top management are made aware of the value of information and their commitment to the principle of managing it as a resource is gained
- policies about information are developed
- line managers are made aware of their responsibilities for information and of its value to them.

Managing information is a continous process which requires a co-ordinated approach across the department.

The benefits of the successful implementation of information management will not only be in the efficient use of information but, more importantly, in making effective use of information to achieve departmental objectives.

An Information Management Function was established to assist the Head of Information Systems in implementing these policies and to:

- 'initiate and develop a data administration function
- and advise on the applicability of data management tools such as data modelling and data dictionary systems.'

H.M. Customs and Excise

Following the Strategic Information Management Study in 1987, the Board of H.M. Customs and Excise has adopted a policy framework for information management which includes these statements:

- 'At every stage of information-related work, the fullest possible account will be taken of corporate information requirements.
- To ensure that information and data are developed in consistent formats and to allow greater ease of access, standards will be developed and adhered to in the following areas:
  - information requirements will be analysed and specified by means of a technique known as soft systems analysis .... [Business Analysis, as described in Annex 2];
  - standard information definitions and descriptions will be agreed, publicised, monitored and controlled;
  - an inventory of information resources will be developed, maintained and publicised.'

and an Information Management Branch has been created to:

- 'develop, maintain, monitor and control these standards
- supply expertise and quality assurance in their application
- review all new project briefs and completed studies which have implications for information management

- identify information gaps and overlaps .... and to indicate existing sources of information which might be relevant to new projects; and
- promote wider departmental awareness of the potential for data sharing .... '

Department of Trade and Industry

In DTI an interdisciplinary Information Management working group has recommended adoption of a policy as follows:

- 'All information held within the DTI is "corporate" and should be available to support all aspects of the work of the department subject only to security or legal restrictions.
- All staff are expected to determine whether information they hold now, or may acquire in the future, is of relevance to others in the department and to make it available.
- All staff are required to keep their information needs under review and, in particular:

  a to check whether any new record or proposed collection of data duplicates or overlaps with existing records or collections of data

  b to be aware of the costs and the benefits of existing or proposed records or data and to reduce costs/increase benefits wherever possible

  c to dispose of data which is no longer needed or to transfer to cheaper storage records for which retrieval within 6 to 24 hours is acceptable

  d to know the cost of providing information to others outside the department, particularly where the department has control or discretion over the amount of information supplied

  e to be aware of the costs to industry, commerce and the public of the information they are required to supply to the department; and

  f to be aware of information that is tradeable and of the opportunities and the departmental processes, for trading in information.'

DTI's draft objectives for Information Management are:

1 'To ensure that DTI has defined its total information requirements and that it keeps those requirements under review, modifying them in the light of changing circumstances.

2 To ensure that the department maintains an up-to-date picture of the information it holds and the sources within the department from which the information can be obtained.

3 To ensure that the department has appropriate mechanisms in place to keep under review its information holdings against its requirements and, where necessary, to dispose of information which is no longer needed.

4 To ensure that the department is aware of external information sources which can be used to obtain information not held internally.

5 To ensure that appropriate storage, retrieval and communication mechanisms are in place to allow information to be moved from its source to the point of need in the most cost-effective manner.

6 To ensure that the department is aware of and takes advantage of opportunities for the wider exploitation of its information resource.'

It is further proposed that the DTI working group's function should be extended to carry out a programme of work to include:

- 'identification of information needs
- mapping of information sources
- identification of redundant information guidelines on managing information for the corporate good
- pointers to managers of information guidance on costs.'

Annex 2 Some methods and techniques

Introduction

Any technique or methodology is only an aid to help in performing some task. Some experienced Consultancy, Inspection and Review (CIR) staff and consultants can get by on their wits alone. For most of us methodologies or techniques can be of great help, properly applied. They:

- give structure to a complex task
- identify the skills — specialist or otherwise — necessary for a piece of work
- produce results in a form intelligible to others
- can be repeated.

There are dangers too:

- Some proprietary methodologies or techniques have been designed for use in the commercial sector and may need to be adapted before they can be used satisfactorily in a Government context
- Methodologies or techniques rigidly applied can cause inflexibility in situations where requirements are subject to change
- The 'standard task' structure of some methodologies or techniques may have the effect of inhibiting creative thinking on the part of those involved in the analytical stages of the exercise.

Techniques and methodologies covered

This Annex does not set out to be an exhaustive survey of methodologies and techniques which may be useful in information management, but those described have all been used, and shown to work in government departments for the tasks we have indicated. Many other equally useful techniques are described in IS Guide A2 Strategic Planning for Information Systems.

Although some of the techniques and methodologies have been designed for use with information in one particular medium, there is considerable scope for using them more widely, and adopting the standard methods of one information service in others. For example, Records Management methods can readily be adopted for electronic filing in Office Automation systems.

It is important to emphasise that none of the techniques or methodologies we have reviewed can be expected to produce, mechanistically, the outputs necessary for successful information management. Their use requires intelligent and skilful staff if worthwhile results are to be obtained.

This annex looks at techniques and methodologies in four areas.

Identifying information needs

Two techniques are included in this section.

The **Business Analysis** technique (BAT) has proved to be particularly effective and economical for defining the broad picture of information needs across the range of a department's operations. The resource commitment involved will, naturally, depend on the size and nature of the department under consideration. In one case a useful and comprehensive high level framework for a department of some 25,000 staff was built up by a team of four within four or five months elapsed time and perhaps 150 man-days of staff resources.

A complementary technique to Business Analysis is **Critical Success Factors** (CSF), which aims to establish those areas in which the organisation under study must perform adequately, or well, in order to be successful.

Identifying information resources

This section describes the method proposed by DTI for carrying out an "information audit", designed originally to identify opportunities for exploiting tradeable information. It has been used successfully in MAFF. Other attempts to compile inventories of information holdings have proved very labour-intensive and costly.

Departments have experience of compiling and maintaining lists of computer systems containing personal data for the purpose of registration under the Data Protection Act. Your departmental library will already have a catalogue of its information. Most departments also have a departmental file list. All these things may be used as initial sources for the total information inventory.

Describing information

The techniques used by different information service specialists are briefly described. Some indication of the scope for exporting the techniques into other information systems work is given, with examples.

Responsibility and accountability for information

In order to allow business managers to assess the relationship between the resources they commit to information handling and the benefit obtained from it, HM Treasury (MSE) has devised a methodology. It is called Cost and Value of Information or CVI.

Techniques identifying information needs

(see paragraphs 3.2 and 3.3)

Business Analysis Technique (BAT)

The business analysis technique described here is based on the Soft Systems methodology that was originated by Professor Peter Checkland at the University of Lancaster, and further developed by commercial consultants. It is designed to provide an understanding of, and solutions to, business problems, especially for defining information systems requirements. It compares the way a business ought to operate in an ideal or "model" sense, with the way that it actually operates in real life, and identifies changes that need to be made.

It has three stages.

Stage I — Producing a Business System Model

The first stage in BAT is to describe the Business System that is needed to achieve the business aims and objectives of the area under study. The business system is not a computer system; it is the whole set of components that must combine to achieve the business aims.

The aim is to produce a model of the department's business, a Business System Model. This is an ideal logical model: the business as it should be. It will not necessarily match the present state of affairs in all respects. It has two components:

- the Business System Definition,
- an Activity Model.

A **Business System Definition (BSD)** is a formal definition of the Business System that sets out what the system is for, what its components are, and how they interact.

A BSD, as a definition of a formal system, must make reference to the following six components, either explicitly or implicitly:

Viewpoint

- The perspective from which this system definition was constructed, which defines the purpose of the system and implies measures of performance

Owner

- The group or individual with responsibility for the system, and with ultimate authority over it

Customer

- The beneficiary (or victim) of the main activities of the system

Actor

- The agents who carry out the main activities of the system

Transformation

- The process that forms the centre of the system's activities; the activity that transforms the system's inputs into its outputs

Environment

- Factors over which the system has no influence, but which affect its performance or impose constraints upon its operation.

It is important to reach agreement on a viewpoint(s). A BSD embodies a particular viewpoint of the area under study. For example, below are two viewpoints or purposes for the Social Security business:

- to provide to the public the benefits laid down in the schemes approved by Parliament, ensuring that contributions are properly paid
- to ensure that those in need receive the necessary funds required for them to sustain a reasonable quality of life, with the minimum of delay.

The viewpoint need not (necessarily) define what is currently going on; it simply represents one perspective on and justification for or purpose of the business or organisation being studied.

The viewpoints adopted will affect the definition of the remaining components of the BSD.

The six components of a well constructed BSD may be remembered by the mnemonic VOCATE.

Below is an example expressing one viewpoint of a school:

V — to promote the moral, intellectual and physical development of young people

O — education authority

C — pupils

A — teaching staff

T — development and presentation of high standard of lessons

E — national curriculum, budget.

This produces the following Business System Definition:

> "An education authority owned system operated by the teaching staff to promote the moral, intellectual and physical development of young people by the development and presentation of good quality lessons, ensuring adherence to the national curriculum and operating within budget."

The next task is to construct an **Activity Model** of each of the business systems that have been defined. Activity models are constructed by asking:

> "What is the minimum set of activities that must logically take place if the business system is to be the one described in the BSD?"

Activity models are built by writing down this set of activities and showing the logical dependencies between them as arrows.

Example of an activity model reflecting the BSD of the school described above is shown in Figure 4.

Whereas the BSD describes what the system *is*, the activity model shows what the system *does*, or needs to do.

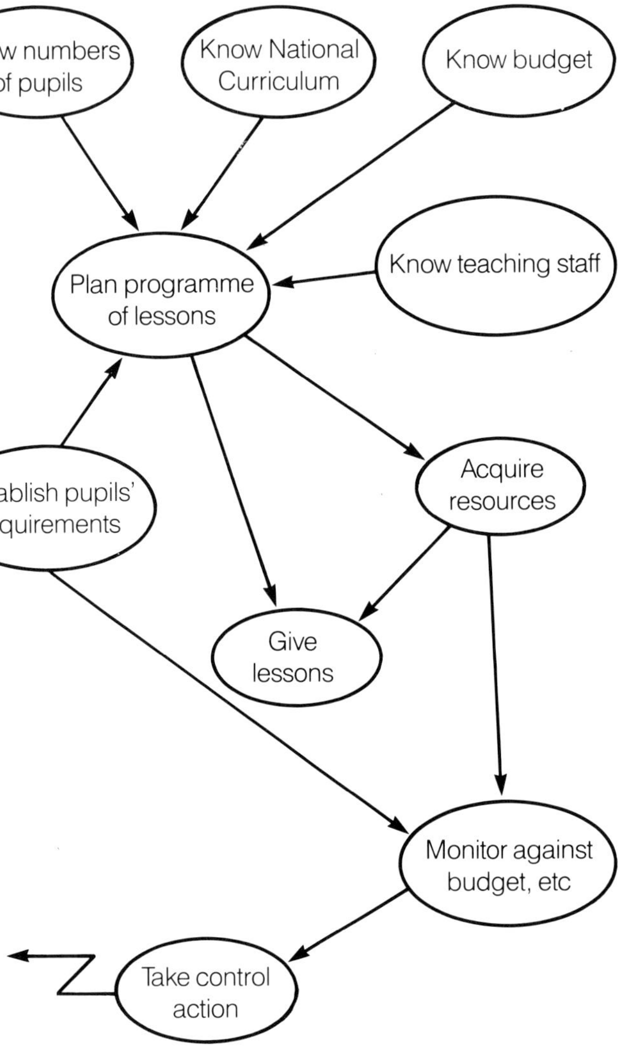

Figure 4 Business System Definition of a school

Different viewpoints are based on different objectives and will generate different sets of activities in the activity models. The total business system model which is used for further, more detailed, work must be formed as a combination of them. The merged model must show all the activities required to achieve all the relevant objectives. It can then be considered to be a picture of the "ideal" business system.

From the information management viewpoint it is clearly essential that a comprehensive single agreed 'target' business system is identified, otherwise the supporting information systems cannot be built. Many of the apparent failures of computer systems have been caused by the failure to make explicit and reconcile the hidden conflicts between the differing viewpoints.

Stage 2 — Characterising the business system

The second stage of the business analysis technique involves describing the final agreed business system in greater detail, by identifying its **key characteristics** and setting out what they ought to be like. Three of the more important characteristics that are relevant to information management problems are the **information** and **communications** required by the business system, and the **organisation structure** that is most appropriate.

In order to identify what information would be needed in the 'target' business system, it is necessary to answer two questions for each activity in the agreed activity model:

- what information is needed in order to carry out this activity? and
- what information is generated by this activity that is used by other activities in the system, or is used outside the system?

The answers to these questions are best set out in a simple table, with columns that show, for each activity, information needed and information generated. Sources and destinations of information (both within and outside the model) can also be added to the tables to show the communications and flows of information needed.

Stage 3 — Measuring and Comparing the actual state of affairs

It is important to emphasise the necessary distinction between the process just described of setting out what the business system ought to be like, and the process that logically follows it, of assessing how well the current situation matches up to this 'ideal'. The first task of this assessment is to find out whether the activities identified in the activity model of the 'target' business system are being carried out. Establish who does what by looking at organisation charts, job descriptions and by interviewing managers. Missing activities, duplicated responsibility for some activities and unnecessary extra activities will quickly be revealed.

For information and communication characteristics, the comparison of the 'ideal' system with the actual involves finding out about the information currently available to staff carrying out the activities, what information systems support exists, and how well the information needs are being met.

The results of these comparisons are conclusions and recommendations about what needs to be changed so that the business can more closely approach the 'ideal' business system that has been described. Clearly, the recommendations may be developed into detailed specification of the information systems needed to support the business or some part of it.

Critical Success Factors (CSFs)

The CSF approach says that, for any organisation, certain areas must perform adequately, or well, if it is to succeed in meeting its business objectives. These areas — the Critical Success Factors — may be either events or activities. They are in a sense the linchpins of the business, and the organisation concerned will need to be able to recognise them and take them as the starting-point for defining information needs and priorities.

The stages in the CSFs technique are:

- Getting the right team together: those involved must, between them, have an understanding of the technique and knowledge of the organisation.

- Identifying and focusing upon aims and objectives in advance of the interviewing programme. This is particularly important when the time available for interviews is constrained, whether by project deadline or because of other demands on interviewees. Possible sources for background information about departmental and divisional aims and objectives are:

  - high-level policy or strategic planning documents
  - submissions to Ministers
  - PES
  - white papers (public expenditure or otherwise)
  - ministerial or other publicly-available statements
  - divisional work plans.

- Developing a (questionnaire-based) interview programme.

- Analysing the information provided during interviews: relating CSFs to stated or implied medium term aims, and deriving information needs from agreed CSFs. It will become clear that the CSFs for one tier of management can be expressed as the objectives for management lower down in the hierarchy.

- Organising a management seminar/workshop to agree the CSFs and information needs.

Because CSFs are, by definition, the key to success for an organisation it is essential that managers should have some means of measuring whether they have been achieved or not. It follows that if information systems are to be relevant to senior managers these systems must support their CSFs.

The CSF technique is best used where the senior management of an organisation are quite clear about what the aims and objectives of the business are, and want to identify the information required to support them.

The CSF approach may be used as part of a wider methodology to determine high-level information strategies, or it can be used on its own to arrive at the information needs of particular groups or individuals inside an organisation. The technique can be particularly useful in helping to arrive at the management information requirements of top and senior management, since it can focus on main aims and objectives, and seeks to identify those key activities which senior managers themselves wish to monitor. It is relatively easy, when their CSFs have been agreed, to prescribe the information they need to judge progress and performance. And it avoids the problem of becoming "bogged down" in a mass of detail not relevant to top management's role.

Some further comments on BAT and CSFs

Both the Business Analysis Technique (BAT) and CSFs have strengths and weaknesses. How, and in which sorts of circumstance, they should each be applied is essentially a matter for the team carrying out the analysis. They will need to judge:

- the purpose of the exercise
- the opportunities for introducing fundamental change and the willingness of top management to effect it
- cost; and
- timing.

Both BAT and CSFs demand a clear statement of the organisation's aims and objectives. Unless this exists already — or has been arrived at either by logical deduction, or by discussion with those who run the organisation — there will be no basis for developing the information structure during the next stage of the exercise. There is, however, a fundamental difference between the two techniques which should be understood and borne in mind at the outset.

The value of BAT is that it offers a structured and rigorous approach to problem-solving in areas where the issues are complex or poorly-defined, and the solutions are far from obvious. It allows a thoroughgoing review of the whole organisation, its systems and its procedures. It therefore goes beyond defining information needs: it helps to define and clarify business objectives; it can be used to cover the tasks of comparison of needs and resources, and suggest action for dealing with mismatches.

Where an organisation's purpose and activities are well-defined and settled, then the CSF approach may be more effective. If top management is quite clear about what the aims and objectives of the business should be, and its concern is simply to decide on the information needed to support those objectives, there is little point in carrying out a wholesale, root-and-branch business analysis. This point is equally relevant in cases where established aims and objectives are perhaps open to challenge — or might at the very least benefit from critical scrutiny. If the review's sponsors have fixed perceptions about how things should be, and have no inclination to alter the status quo, the demand will be for a technique which recognises these constraints, but which is still able to provide a clear and effective way forward. In circumstances like these, CSFs can offer a straightforward and pragmatic approach to problem-solving, without the kind of investment in time and effort that would be demanded by BAT.

Techniques for identifying information resources

(see paragraph 3.4)

Information audit

The general approach for carrying out a departmental information audit should be as follows:

a Begin by examining the department as an input-output system. Identify the raw data that is collected, and the environment in which it is assembled, manipulated and refined. Identify the key "owners" of that data.

b Review output data to see what value is added by the department to the raw information it receives. This may help to identify data with potential for commercial exploitation (see section 3.10.1 'Tradeable Information'). Ascertain the internal and external purposes for which the information is acquired or produced.

c Identify the sub-systems which have been created within the department to ease information-handling, and which serve particular units or functions. These may be purely indexing or abstracting services intended for specific local requirements, but they may nonetheless be of value in an altogether different context.

d Develop a clear and consistent set of criteria for describing the content, structure and technical features of the various information systems.

e Establish the currency of the information held, the frequency with which it is updated, and the effort and cost associated with updating it.

f Identify the key information handlers, ie those people at working level who understand the information resources and who can act as contact points for advice on particular systems.

Gathering the data

A questionnaire (with optional interview) structured to elicit the information required for the inventory records is a particularly effective means of data-collection. It should be circulated throughout the organisation and directed at staff at the appropriate level, which will usually be branch or divisional head. Those answering the questionnaire should be asked to think carefully about their information 'systems' in the broadest sense. Some systems will readily come to mind, either because they are high-profile, or because they are used regularly; others will not be quite so obvious, but it is just as important for these to be covered by the questionnaire responses. Questions could usefully address the following aspects of the organisation's information resources:

Content

— Name of information-collection system or title of database.

— Purpose for which used, and details of subjects covered.

Management

— Whether the system is external or internal. If internal, what the current state of development is; what, if any, further enhancements are planned.

— How often data is received and/or updated.

— How old data is by the time users obtain it.

Availability

— Who has access to and use of the information. Whether there are secondary users, and, if so, the terms of their access. Whether on-line access is available, or, if not, whether that is technically feasible; whether paper reports or printouts are available.

Contact

— Who can provide advice and answers to enquiries.

Commercial exploitability

— Extent of present commercial exploitation, if any; potential for further exploitation.

— What refinement/processing is needed to enable this to happen.

Form

— How the information is held: the physical medium (paper, registered files, computer databases, reference books, directories, microfilm, photographic, etc).

— Technical considerations (system specifications, hardware and software, system manager etc).

Size

— How large the information collection is (eg, number of registered files, index cards, megabytes of data).

The questionnaire-points outlined above are for guidance only; in practice, the structure of the questionnaire and the precise wording of each question must obviously depend upon the details required for the inventory. The initial survey itself should be followed up with personal interviews with staff at all levels to enable them, where necessary, to clarify and elaborate upon the information they have provided.

Organising the inventory

The data obtained from the information inventory audit constitutes the raw material for the departmental information inventory. The inventory must be organised carefully if it is to be of value as a comprehensive catalogue of all the information sources inside the department. Unlike a traditional library catalogue, however, the departmental information inventory will generally be concerned only with information "groups" (ie, discrete collections of data), and not with individual items (eg, a single file, book or video film).

A typical or "model" inventory record ought, as a minimum, to contain the following particulars:

Name/title

- Name of information group; title of file series or database.

Subject

- An indication of the intellectual content of material. This may include either an abstract or relevant indexing terms (which could be selected from a controlled vocabulary).

Use

- The purpose the information is intended to serve.

Location/access point

- An indication of where and how the information may be accessed, and by whom.

Producer responsible

- The person or agency responsible for the information, and the name of the person to contact for further details.

Physical details

- A description of the medium on which the information is held, and other technical particulars.

Currency

- The age of data and how often it is updated.

Computer Systems support for the inventory

A department may, of course, choose to vary slightly or add to the category headings suggested above to suit its own requirements.

It will probably be most sensible to manage and manipulate the inventory as a computer database. The storage and retrieval of information contained within it will then be both quick and relatively simple. Each information group will be held as a single database record; and its unique details will be set out under appropriate category headings arranged in a standard format. A number of software packages are available commercially for this purpose.

In computer systems, information may be organised using software tools such as a database management system, or a data dictionary. Data dictionaries may be used within a database management system, or alone, to catalogue collections of computer files, and the data items. The Information Manager (see paragraph 2.4) may use these existing records to discover what databases exist, what data they hold and what information can be pulled from them and how they may be accessed. A data dictionary could be used, with suitable naming standards, to hold the complete information inventory for the department's paper records and computer records.

Databases

A database is a common collection of stored data so structured that the requirements of many programs and applications can be met. Although in the past they were written from the ground up using a high level language such as Cobol or Pascal, they are now developed with the use of Database Management System (DBMS) packages. A DBMS is the software which handles the storage and retrieval of data in a database. It also includes other facilities such as the maintenance of security and the integrity of data.

Most databases will have been written to serve the needs of a particular group of users (senior management or one area of business) and will only be accessible through computer systems which are specific to those users. Some will only provide hard copy (paper) output to their customer group, normally because the interface language is not easy to learn and use and access will only be available through the data processing unit. Others may allow users (perhaps a wide range of users) to query the database directly, using on-line terminals and a special query language (SQL). This latter is becoming the norm — indeed it is now mandatory for all Relational Database Management Systems to come complete with SQL to the appropriate standard.

Data Dictionaries

A data dictionary is a facility for maintaining descriptions about the data held by an organisation. Typically it records the names, descriptions, size and structure of each data item. Data dictionaries were developed mainly to ensure standards in data naming conventions and to enable the impact of proposed changes to the database to be analysed.

In its simplest form, the data dictionary may be a list of data items and definitions kept on paper in a folder. At the other end of the spectrum it will include:

- the latest information (automatically up-dated as the database develops) about the data structure (in a relational database the tables, and possibly the file and records as well, together with their relationships)
- the users
- security (access rights) and integrity rules
- complete definitions of every screen form, report, graph, chart and application.

The information in a data dictionary is normally stored as a database itself. Its structure will depend on the product. If it has been specifically designed to manage a particular database product then it will usually have the same structure as that database (the dictionary supporting a relational database will, for example, be presented as two-dimensional tables), but there is no guarantee of this. An interface will be available providing access in order to question, manipulate and modify the dictionary; but the language may not be particularly user-friendly, and a working knowledge of the database it supports will almost certainly be necessary.

Techniques for describing information

It is necessary to find a way of naming the subject matter of information so that different types of information can be referred to consistently at all stages. For example, the naming terminology ('description language') used to draw up the information inventory should be the same as that used to define the business's needs for information. The information inventory itself will list many sources of information, and that information may exist in different forms (papers, books, computer records, photographs, etc); but the subject matter will be similar in many cases, and must always be capable of being searched for, regardless of its source or form. Internal consistency of terminology in the inventory is essential for two reasons:

- duplications can be identified; and
- the inventory itself can be integrated and understood by many types of enquirer.

The technique for describing information is called **indexing.** The different approaches to indexing that are availble are outlined briefly below. A greater or lesser degree of precision and control can be imposed by different methods of indexing.

Approaches to indexing

Indexing is the shorthand expression of the ideas contained in a document or other information source.

Concept or **subject indexing** involves analysing the subject matter of a document, and choosing appropriate terms to represent it. The effectiveness of subject indexing as a means of identifying and retrieving the material required by users depends upon having a properly constructed index language. The choice of the right index terms, and the systematic arrangement of those terms, are therefore tasks which need careful thought. This is true whether or not the index is handled, and enquiries are made, using a computer.

By contrast, **word indexing** is a description of the document as a whole by reference to individual words or phrases which occur in the text. The index to be found at the back of a book is an example of a word or phrase index in its simplest form.

Free-text indexing

This is a form of word indexing. Documents are read or keyed onto a database, either in full, or as self-contained summaries or abstracts. Every word, except for short or common ones which may be excluded, then becomes an index term for the document in which it occurs. In searching, the free-text retrieval software interrogates the index and locates those documents which contain the chosen search-term(s) in whatever context they happen to be present. With many of the software retrieval packages now available, this search process can be refined by:

- restricting the search to a named field within the document eg. title;
- using Boolean logic (ie, the use of the operators 'and', 'or' and 'not') to combine search terms; or
- both together.

Natural language

This is a form of free-text (word) indexing in which only pre-selected terms are indexed. It can be applied to either manual or computer-based systems. Indexing terms may be taken from the document title or heading, from an appended indexing field, from an abstract or from the main text itself. Although the selection process is straightforward and involves relatively little document analysis, natural language indexing will not necessarily result in effective retrieval unless the index terms are very carefully selected.

Controlled vocabulary

This is a form of concept indexing. Controlled vocabulary indexing involves constructing a set of approved terms to describe all the concepts encompassed within a particular subject area. From this prescribed list, index terms, or 'descriptors', are assigned to each information item. Vocabulary control ensures a measure of discipline and consistency in the indexing process, and can help to avoid the retrieval problems that might arise, for example, from the indiscriminate use of synonyms. It can take the form of either:

- a straightforward list of prescribed or authorised terms; or
- a thesaurus.

Indexing with a thesaurus

A thesaurus is a controlled vocabulary in which the indexing terms are arranged hierarchically to show the logical relationships between them. The usual relationships are:

- synonym (equivalent)
- broader term (higher level)
- narrower term (lower level) and
- related term (similar).

A thesaurus can serve as a very useful aid to the detailed analysis of information content. It allows the same information held in different sources to be described consistently, and can therefore be applied equally to books, registered files and other non-bibliographic information media. Retrieval of a particular item of information will depend upon the terms which the indexer has allocated to it from the thesaurus. There is no theoretical limit to the number of terms that can be used: in this, as in other areas, judgement is required in deciding on the level of detail necessary to ensure that users' needs are met.

A number of thesauri have been developed in government, (a well-known example is used in POLIS, the Parliamentary document database) and some of these have been published. There are a few which are of general application, but most have been tailored to suit a particular group of enquirers and are therefore limited in their subject scope. Standard or 'off-the-shelf' thesauri are unlikely to satisfy the specific needs of any government department, but the development of a customised thesaurus can be a long and intellectually-demanding exercise which may require the specialist skills of someone like a professional librarian. Nevertheless, in a scientific, technical or any other specialised environment, a well-structured thesaurus can provide the effective vocabulary control without which any retrieval system — computer-based or manual — will be unable to function fully and effectively.

A thesaurus can best be developed, controlled and maintained on a computer. If it is to be paper-based, some thought should be given to the question of managing and providing access to the volume of printed material that will accumulate as new terms are added and existing ones are reorganised. Where the thesaurus is held on computer and is available via on-line display, this will not be a problem, but it will still be important to be able to amend and manipulate the constituent terms as and when necessary.

Examples of indexing in practice

The library catalogue

The information inventory to be found in the library is the catalogue, which holds details of every item (book, periodical, report, etc.) in stock. A traditional card catalogue will be arranged in alphabetical order of author's name or title or subject. The field chosen for ordering a card catalogue is significant since that becomes the "key" for retrieving the items. With a computerised catalogue many fields on the record may be searchable and used in combination for retrieval.

A library catalogue record will usually contain:

- publisher
- publication date
- author
- number of pages
- classification number (implying shelf location)
- number of pages; and
- indexing terms.

The terms used by the librarian to describe content will normally be derived from both a classification scheme and from a related vocabulary of indexing terms. The classification scheme is used primarily for logical and physical location of items; the index terms are used by enquirers to identify items which are relevant to their area of interest or work.

A library-style catalogue of computer files

A project was carried out by the Computer Files Cataloguing Group (CFCG) under the aegis of the Economic and Social Research Council, using trained librarians to catalogue computer files. The exercise is part of a broad strategy to encourage wider access to, and exploitation of, machine-readable databases. The CFCG's task was:

- to identify and develop cataloguing standards for computer files
- to implement a trial union catalogue; and
- to disseminate the Group's work to a wider audience.

The outcome of the Group's work was the publication in October 1988 of a draft report entitled 'Guide to cataloguing computer files in the UK: a practical guide to standards'. The Guide brings together a number of references to terms and practices recommended for describing material involving computer files. The approach has been to follow and extend the well-established library conventions used to create catalogue records for books, periodicals and other items requiring systematic bibliographic control.

The Guide concentrates on defining relevant descriptive fields of information about computer files. These fields are organised for cataloguing purposes under four broad headings:

- identification and availability
- subject and content
- physical characteristics and technical information; and
- access and management information.

The Guide does not attempt to address the problem of entering catalogue information into cataloguing software, or of the retrieval and display of the catalogue information.

Paper records management

In the registry the description of the content or subject matter of paper records has a similarly long history and a number of tried and trusted techniques have been established. The two most common ones are the **hierarchical** and **co-ordinate** themes schemes. Both schemes are designed to manage files and collections of papers covering the same topic, but not individual papers; they might easily be applied to electronic files and documents. Either scheme may be handled manually or be computer-supported.

Hierarchical

Under this scheme files are identified by their primary and secondary subjects. The terms used to describe subjects are taken from a pre-defined hierarchy of descriptors of, at the highest or primary level, areas of general or global interest and, at the next or secondary level, topics of specific concern within those areas. A third or tertiary descriptor is then added to identify the file uniquely. The descriptors taken together form the file title and the number which is allocated to each provides file notation (a unique reference number).

This system is most useful where the nature of the work does not change and subject areas can be predicted. Once the hierarchy of terms has been defined the scheme is easy to use, but retrieval may be slow since the tertiary element tends to grow unchecked.

Co-ordinate themes

Under this scheme files are classified on the subject matter of their title, the terms being derived from a departmental list. Theoretically there is no limit to the number of terms which may be used, but for manual systems it is normally restricted to two or three. Each term or combination of terms is numbered, enabling file series and notation to be constructed.

Retrieval depends on creating and maintaining an alphabetical index of the subject terms. Because new themes can be added to the list relatively easily, this system is extremely useful in areas where the nature of the work tends to change. The co-ordinate theme system tends to be more difficult to use than the hierarchical scheme, but retrieval is much quicker.

Local accountability for managing the information resource

The cost and value of information

To manage any resource the manager must plan, monitor and control his or her use of the resource. To enable departments and line managers to take responsibility for their expenditure on information and information services, and for the quality of the information they are required to supply to others, the costs of information must be made visible and be measured in relation to the value which they and their customers obtain from it.

To assist with this the Management Systems and Efficiency Division of HM Treasury have produced a methodology called 'Cost and Value of Information' (CVI) for defining the cost and value of information outputs.

The methodology is outlined in Figure 5. A detailed description of each step is included in the guide to the methodology, and what follows is only a brief account of the process.

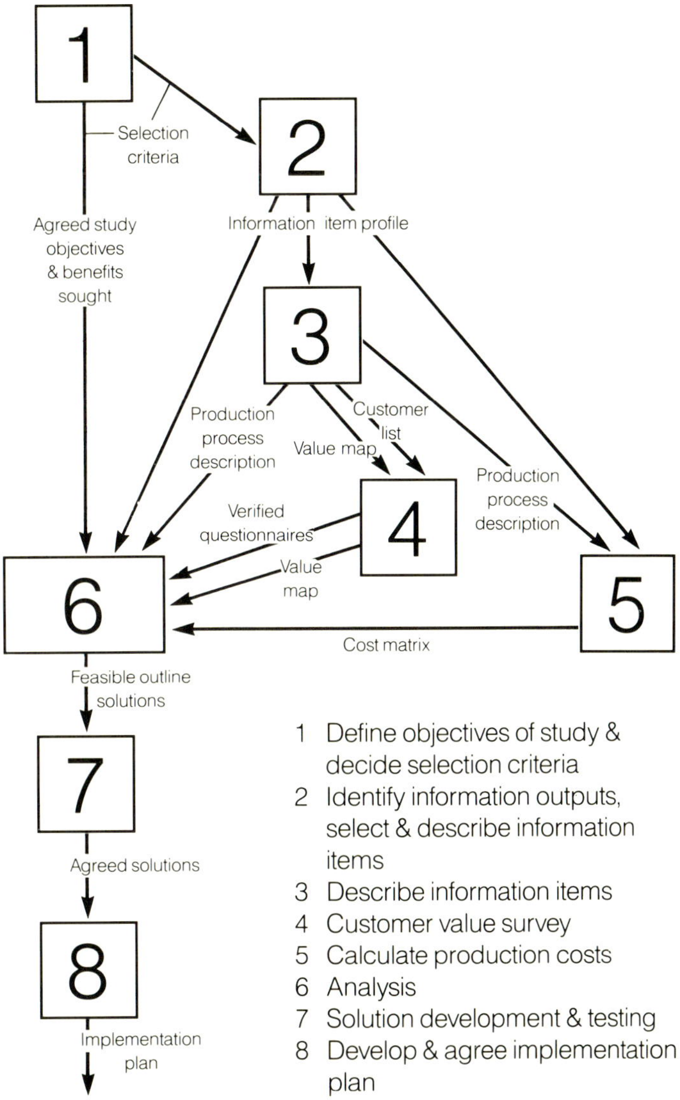

Figure 5 Cost and Value of Information methodology

The methodology is designed for use by the managers of business units with the assistance of experienced Management Services staff in close collaboration with unit staff. The methodology focuses on the unit's information outputs. It is not concerned with internal communications; only recorded information which is passed to people outside the unit, the customers, is considered.

At an initial meeting the information output by the unit is identified; the objectives of the study are determined in the light of the agreed aims of the unit and these objectives are then used to decide the selection criteria for choosing which of the information outputs will be studied in detail.

The costs of the production process of each chosen item are calculated and its values established. As cash equivalence is rarely possible to define for an information product, no attempt is made to specify the value of the chosen items in cash terms. Instead the customers are asked, either in interview or by written questionnaire, to assess their value in use, that is the value of each item to them in their work.

It is then necessary to analyse and compare the costs and values that have been established, looking for discrepancies between the producers' and their customers' view of the value of an item, and deciding whether costs are not considered too high in relation to perceived values. The methodology provides assistance with this step in the form of a diagnostic checklist, but it must be used with care; analysis is not a mechanistic process and considerable judgement must be used. Where discrepencies are found, or if costs are considered to be too high, the manager must decide whether to reduce costs or to improve value. Finally a course of action to implement the manager's decision, acceptable to both producers and customers is planned and implemented.

Annex 3 External sources of information

Commercial databases

There has been a significant growth in recent years in the number of commercial companies whose business is to sell information to public or other private sector customers, usually through a direct on-line link to the subscriber's own computer terminal. (Copies on disc, tape or CD-ROM of the database, or extracts from them may sometimes be purchased).

Subject areas covered by on-line databases are many and varied, but fall into a number of broad categories:

- scientific and technical
- legal
- financial services
- news/current affairs services; and parliamentary.

The main types of database are:

- numeric (financial statistical data, arithmetic manipulation, tables/graphics)
- bibliographic (references/summaries/abstracts of books, periodicals etc)
- full text (complete journal articles or other text items)
- referral (on-line directories of bibliographical or other information).

Access to on-line commercial databases is usually through departmental libraries. Advice on their structure and content is provided by the professional library staff who use them as alternatives to printed sources. Searching can be as broad or as specific as necessary, and data retrieved can be tailored to suit users' requirements. Data is almost always available as a printout.

Methods of charging for the use of on-line databases vary from company to company. In some cases, the subscriber makes a single, up-front payment which entitles him to unlimited use; in others, the practice is to charge on a per-transaction or connect-time basis. Generally, however, such costs are more than offset by the savings in the time of both the user and the professional staff who access the system.

Press cuttings services

Much information about the issues which affect, and are affected by, the work of a department is produced by the press and the broadcast media.

Extracts of relevant articles published in the national and regional newspapers, in journals, in magazines and in other periodicals can be obtained from commercial press cuttings services through either your Departmental Library or your Press and Information Office. The costs of these services vary, and it is important to ensure that the one that is chosen has a proper understanding of the Department's business, and is able to identify material which is relevant to its needs and interests. Press cuttings services can also provide verbatim transcripts of selected sections of radio and television programmes.

All Government news releases issued through Central Office of Information's News Distribution Service are now available on PROFILE, the Financial Times on-line Information Service. Two services are available:

- HERMES contains a full archive of all releases, is up-dated overnight and available from 0800 daily. This material is available permanently.
- HERMES DAILY contains only those releases issued the previous day and is available from 0800 daily.

Surveys

Surveys may be made on a regular basis (eg. the census and Family Expenditure Survey), or specially commissioned to discover specific information required, for example, to formulate policy (eg. about the nature or extent of some problem in the environment or the public perception of an issue). The Survey Control Unit of the Central Statistical Office is the central focus for all surveys, and advice should be sought from the unit before any survey is undertaken.

Grey literature

A substantial and growing body of valuable information exists in the form of semi-published or 'grey' literature. This can broadly be defined as 'written material which is not available through normal bookselling channels'. The term covers a wide range of items: for example, technical reports, research papers, translations, theses, pre-prints, and official publications on all subjects.

Grey literature is, by its very nature, difficult to identify and to obtain. The patterns of production, distribution and bibliographic control are fundamentally different from those which operate for mainstream published literature. Typical characteristics are small print runs and non-professional standards of editing and production. Furthermore, because it bypasses conventional publication channels, grey literature tends to be poorly publicised and catalogued, and as a result is not generally available through normal library services.

Grey literature remains, nonetheless, an important public asset. The range of subjects it covers is extensive, and the information it contains will often be more detailed than that to be found in conventional published literature. It is likely, moreover, to be of interest to a wider readership than the one for which it was primarily intended. This will obviously be true, for example, in the fields of technological, scientific and medical research. Information users who are serious about exploiting all sources of material relevant to their work — wherever they are to be found — should therefore be aware of, and respond to, the potential offered by grey literature.

Internationally, there are a number of organisations concerned with promoting knowledge about and exploitation of grey literature in all its forms. In Britain, the British Library Document Supply Centre has built up a substantial worldwide collection of reports, translations, academic theses, supplementary publications, local government reports and semi-published conference proceedings going back over 25 years. The Centre indexes around 15,000 British items each year. Material is obtained in a number of ways: through exchange agreements and special acquisition arrangements with producers, from British embassies abroad, from university libraries, and via collecting agents with specialist knowledge of particular subjects. Non-HMSO official publications, for example, are collected and indexed by the publishing firm Chadwyck-Healey (see below).

Catalogue of United Kingdom Official Publications

A comprehensive catalogue of all UK official publications (UKOP) is produced jointly by HMSO and Chadwyck-Healey Ltd, and is available to subscribers on CD-ROM. It is intended for users of every type of library — public, academic, research or commercial — with a need to identify and obtain publications from official sources. The Catalogue includes both official documents produced by HMSO and those published independently by Government organisations (including all departments). It also contains records of publications of international organisations, including the EEC, UN, UNESCO and OECD.

UKOP covers all material from 1980 to date, and is updated quarterly. The use of CD-ROM as a storage medium means that the database is accessible through a personal computer, and that searching for and retrieval of information can be done quickly and accurately.

Any government organisation wishing to have its non-HMSO publications included in UKOP should make the necessary arrangements with Chadwyck-Healey through its own librarian.

Annex 4 HMSO Publication Services

HMSO is now an agency, and operates like any other commercial publishing company. It funds directly most of the publication which it undertakes for departments, but has agreements with a few organisations to publish for them on an agency basis. Where a publishing project is judged to be commercially viable, HMSO will meet in full the cost of the following:

- design
- production
- marketing and publicity
- storage; and
- distribution.

HMSO's publishing service extends from the receipt of a manuscript or camera-ready copy through to the printing and publication of finished copies. From the sponsoring department's point of view, it is often a good idea for HMSO to become involved as early as possible in the process so that it can provide advice on matters such as:

- preparation of camera-ready copy
- market potential
- form and structure of the publication
- number of words
- need for and use of colour; and preparation of illustrations, drawings and diagrams.

HMSO also provide editorial and proof-reading services, by using either its own staff or external consultants with the relevant knowledge or expertise. Other specialist HMSO staff are involved in copy writing, and in the promotion of published material through advertising, press and media coverage and direct-mail publicity.

Editorial services and advice on certain technical aspects of publication are normally provided free of charge to sponsoring departments. The cost to the sponsor is limited to the cost of copies of the publication bought for official use and for resale. These copies are supplied at a range of discounts according to the terms of the purchase.

HMSO will negotiate payment of royalties on the sales of all publications produced on behalf of the sponsoring department. The amount of royalty in each case will depend largely on market considerations. Final responsibility for setting the sale price will rest with HMSO as publisher.

Annex 5 Sources of Help and Advice

General

For more information on the contents of this publication contact:

Your Departmental Support Manager or The Information Systems Strategy Unit

Central Computer and Telecommunications Agency
Riverwalk House
157–161 Millbank
LONDON SW1P 4RT
Telephone 071 217 3000

Records management

The Records Management Programme, run by Management and Personnel Office, produced a series of guidance notes on the management of records and registries. These are now available from:

The Publishing Unit
HM Treasury
Treasury Chambers
Parliament Street
LONDON SWl
Telephone 071 270 5195

The responsibilities of Departmental Records Officers, in relation to the permanent archive of historical records as required by the Public Records Acts, are set out in the Departmental Records Office's Guide, published by the Public Record Office. Contact your DRO or the PRO.

The Records Management Society has a specialist interest group for organisations covered by the Public Records Act (OPRA).

Library Services

Contact your departmental Librarian for information and assistance with any of the following:

- access to, and charging arrangements for, commercial online databases
- describing information, including the use of cataloguing techniques and the development of thesauri and other forms of controlled vocabulary

- access to, and indexing of, departmental and other official publications **not** published through HMSO

- using information sources, and systematic bibliographic subject searching.

Surveys

The Survey Control Unit of the Central Statistical Office can—and, in most circumstances, should—assist with special surveys:

Central Statistical Office
Survey Control Unit
Great George Street
London SW1

Government News Releases—Retrieval/ Archive Service

Further information on this service can be obtained from:

Archive Service
Press Office
Central Office of Information
Hercules House
Hercules Road
London SE1 7DU
Telephone 071 261 8247 *or*

COI News Distribution Service
Telephone 071 261 8527

Grey Literature

Further information and advice on this is available from:

Deputy Director
British Library Document Supply Centre,
Boston Spa
Wetherby, West Yorkshire LS23 7BQ
Telephone 0937 843434

UK Official Publications (UKOP)

Further advice and information about UKOP may be obtained from:

HMSO Books
Publications Centre
51 Nine Elms Lane
London SW8 5DR
Telephone 071 873 8401

Computer Files Cataloguing Group (CFCG)

For further information about the CFCG Guide and its use contact:

Peter Burnhill
University of Edinburgh
Data Library and Computing Service
Main Library Building
George Square
Edinburgh EH8 9LJ
Telephone 031 667 1011 extn 4371/2

Imagery Resources

For advice on information management of imagery resources (primarily still photographs) the contacts are:

Department of Information Studies and Technology
Ealing College of Higher Education
St Mary's Road
Ealing
London W5 5RF
Telephone 081 579 5000
or

British Association of Picture Libraries and Agencies
13 Woodberry Crescent
London N10 1PJ
Telephone 081 883 2531

CCTA general advice on Information Systems

CCTA publishes guidance on all matters concerning the management and development of Information Systems in a series of guides, the 'IS Guides'. These guides are supplemented by more frequently updated information in the CCTA's IS Notices. These publications are available through your IT Directorate or:

IS Notices
CCTA
Riverwalk House
157–161 Millbank
London SW1P 4RT

IS Guides
John Wiley & Sons Ltd
Baffins Lane
Chichester
West Sussex PO19 1UD

The current list of IS Guides is:

A1 An Introduction to Information Systems in Government
A2 Strategic Planning for Information Systems
A3 Computer and Office Systems Planning
A4 Telecommunications Planning
A5 A Project Manager's Guide

B1 The Users' Role in System Development
B2 The Feasibility Study
B3 The Full Study
B4 Appraising Investment in Information Systems
B5 The Operational Requirement
B6 Procurement
B7 Evaluation
B8 Systems Engineering

C1 Services Management
C2 Environmental Services
C3 Contingency Planning
C4 Security and Privacy
C5 Telecommunications Operation and Management
C6 Capacity Planning
C7 Availability Planning

D1 Small Systems
D2 Microcomputer Systems and Software
D3 Office System Facilities

E1 The Information Systems Services Industry
E2 The Hire and Management of Consultants
E3 Turnkey Projects
E4 Facilities Management

Methods and Techniques

Further information about the methods and techniques described in this guide is available from CT1, CCTA.

Training in the techniques is provided through the Civil Service College.

Telephone 071 834 6644

HMSO Publication

For further information about HMSO's publishing service and for advice about Crown Copyright, the contact is:

HMSO
St Crispins
Duke Street
Norwich NR3 1PD
Telephone 0603 622211

Tradeable Information

For further information about the Tradeable Information Initiative, the contact is:

Derrick Porter
Department of Trade and Industry
Kingsgate House
66–74 Victoria Street
London SE1E 6SW
Telephone 071 215 2654 or 071 215 2632

Further reading

Data Protection Act

Departmental Security Instructions

Journals:

- Government Computing
- State Librarian
- International Journal of Information Management
- Records Management Quarterly
- MPO guidelines on Records Management
- Information Management Review

Annex 6 Glossary of Terms

Aims	The long term business goals of the department (compare 'objectives').
BSD	Business System Definition. See Annex 2
Business Strategy	A definition of a department's future business direction, needs and objectives, and the resources required to meet them. In departments comprising many separate 'business units', a business strategy might be developed for each. Those strategies would be brought together into a corporate strategy.
CD–ROM	Read Only Memory: computer data kept on compact discs, which can only be 'read' by a computer but not altered by it.
CSFs	Critical Success Factors. See Annex 2
data and information	Information is applied data, that is to say that when raw data is presented to a user, at the point of its use, it becomes information. Data has potential value, information is valuable.
database	A structured organisation of records, for purposes such as automatically generating up-to-date reports, and answering ad hoc queries.
data dictionary	A listing of all the names of all items of data in a computer database, with other selected information about each item.
DBMS	Database management system, the software which handles the storage and retrieval of data in a computer database.
information management	'The means by which an organisation maximises the efficiency with which it plans, collects, organises, uses, controls, disseminates and disposes of its information

and through which it ensures that the value and potential value of that information is identified and exploited to the fullest extent.'

Or, in short, managing information as a resource is concerned with getting 'value for money from information'.

Data management, records management, and library management are all aspects of information management, ie activities involved in managing information.

information system — Any procedure or process, with or without IT support, which provides a way of acquiring, storing, processing, or disseminating information.

IS — Information system

IT — Information technology

Information technology — Any use of equipment to provide an information system.

IS Planning Secretariat — A central team providing support to the IS Steering Committee and co-ordinating the activities of the Executive Committees. The team is responsible for definition (in accordance with IS Steering Committee wishes), monitoring and review of the IS Strategy.

IS Steering Committee — The top management group responsible for the direction of information systems in a department. It commissions, directs, and agrees the IS Strategy.

IS Strategy — A formal definition of the intended future deployment of IS, and its supporting policies, programmes of work and infrastructure within a department in support of business objectives.

Management and Technical Policies — These policies form part of the IS Strategy. They provide the backbone of guidance required by users and those responsible for progressing the Strategy.

management information	One category of information. It is that information which enables managers to assess the effectiveness and efficiency, etc. of their areas of business.
megabyte	Approximately one million bytes, or characters, of data.
Objectives	The measurable milestones which mark progress towards achieving the department's aims.
on-line computer system	A computer system that can be accessed system remotely by users via a communications link and which provides an immediate response.
PES	Public Expenditure Survey.
query language	A set of messages, understood by a computer system, which enable users to retrieve data from the computer's database. Frequently it is not necessary for the user to know, or be aware of, the query language because messages are conveyed automatically by using some prearranged routine convenient to users (for example by using prescribed keys on a keyboard).
relational database	A type of computer database having a particular kind of structure which enables users to retrieve the data in a flexible way.
SQL	Structured Query Language, a query language for relational databases.

Printed in the United Kingdom for HMSO.
Dd.0292773, 8/90, C10, 3385/4, 5673, 111303.